Animals in Danger

Acknowledgments

Executive Editor: Diane Sharpe
Supervising Editor: Stephanie Muller
Design Manager: Sharon Golden
Page Design: Ian Winton
Photography: Bruce Coleman: cover (left, bottom right), pages 9, 10, 18, 20-21, 22-23, 25, 27; Oxford Scientific Films: pages 13, 17; Tony Stone: cover (top right), pages 7, 14.

Library of Congress Cataloging-in-Publication Data

Herschell, Michael.
    Animals in danger/Michael Herschell; illustrated by Jenny Mumford.
        p.   cm. — (Read all about it)
    Includes index.
    ISBN 0-8114-5732-X Hardcover
    ISBN 0-8114-3773-6 Softcover
    1. Endangered species — Juvenile literature.   [1. Endangered species.] I. Mumford, Jenny, ill. II. Title.
III. Series: Read all about it (Austin, Tex.)
QL83.H47 1995
591.52'9—dc20

                                      94-30273
                                        CIP
                                        AC

2 3 4 5 6 7 8 9 0 PO 00 99 98 97 96 95

Animals in Danger

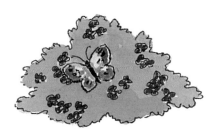

Michael Herschell

Illustrated by
Jenny Mumford

STECK-VAUGHN
COMPANY
ELEMENTARY · SECONDARY · ADULT · LIBRARY

We're at the zoo.

We want to find out about endangered animals.

Animals are endangered if they begin slowly dying out. Many animals are even in danger of becoming extinct.

5

At this zoo, we care for
endangered animals.

Why are some
animals in danger?

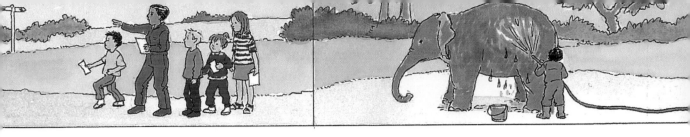

Animals can become endangered for many different reasons. Sometimes it can be because the area where they live is destroyed. This is called habitat destruction.

That's what is happening to the rain forests.

This animal is called a lemur. Lemurs live in Madagascar, which is an island near Africa.

Are lemurs endangered?

8

Yes, their rain forests are being cut down to make room so farmers can grow crops.

We should help the farmers grow crops without cutting down the rain forests.

9

I know what this animal is.
It's a giant panda.

Giant pandas live in China. They mainly eat bamboo plants. But the bamboo there is being burned and cleared for farmland.

> We should save the bamboo that the giant pandas eat.

Look at that little frog!

This kind of tree frog lives in the swamps of Florida.

12

The tree frog needs damp air so its skin doesn't dry out. But too many people are draining the swamps to make more farmland.

We should make sure people always leave enough swampland for the frogs.

Sometimes animals are killed by pollution. Many other animals are endangered because of hunting.

14

This kind of seal was once hunted.
Now they are protected in most countries
where they live.

The cubs are
so beautiful.

Otters are endangered all over the world. This is partly because of hunting and partly because the rivers and oceans where they live are being polluted.

16

We must keep people from polluting the rivers and oceans.

This is a black rhinoceros. Black rhinos are endangered because hunters called poachers kill them just to get their horns.

18

These are the tigers. They are endangered, too.

Why are they endangered?

Tigers are hunted for their fur, and the forests where they live are destroyed for farmland.

20

Today, many tigers are protected by Project Tiger and live in special preserves.

The tiger is my favorite animal in the zoo!

21

Jaguars are hunted because they are so beautiful. Some people want to use their fur to make coats.

24

It's a cockatoo. Cockatoos are in danger because collectors trap them in the rain forests and sell them for pets.

We should stop people from selling endangered animals.

25

Are any insects endangered, too?

26

Yes, this butterfly is called a large blue.

The pastures where the large blue lives
are being destroyed. Also, collectors
have netted so many that this butterfly is
nearly extinct.

Thank you for our day at this special zoo.

We learned so much about endangered animals.

You can do many things to help animals in danger.

You can join a local wildlife group.
You can plant a wild garden.
You can choose not to buy things made
from endangered animals.

Can you remember the names of these endangered animals? The answers are on the last page, but don't look until you have tried naming all the animals.

1.

2.

3.

4.

5.

6.

7.

Index

Answers: 1. Tiger 2. Seal 3. Lemur 4. Giant panda 5. Cockatoo
6. Large blue butterfly 7. Tree frog